The Air Fryer Cookbook for Beginners

Super-Easy and Delicious Recipes Complete with Nutritions and Full Recipe Lists incl. Lunchtime Inspirations

Simon C. Garfield

ISBN - 9798351503578

Table of Contents

EXCLUSIVE BONUS

40 Weight Loss Recipes

&

14 Days Meal Plan

Scan the QR-Code and receive
the FREE download:

Introduction

If you have an air fryer, you are probably always looking for new ways to use your device to make delicious, crispy, and healthy food for the whole family, no matter what time of day or what day of the week. Fortunately, air fryers are versatile and allow you to make all kinds of meals – not just chips / fries!

It's a great idea to use your air fryer regularly so you can make the most of the gadget and the health boost it offers. To be clear before starting, food is not automatically healthy just because it has been cooked in an air fryer. It often still contains quite a high level of fat, and many air fryer foods (e.g. chips / fries, waffles, bacon, doughnuts, steaks, and more) are not particularly healthy. However, using an air fryer is much better for you than deep frying your meals, so if you're a fan of fried meals, it's definitely a better option because it will massively reduce the amount of oil that is in your food.

This can have major health benefits, and is an ideal option if you are struggling to reduce your dependence on fried foods. Instead of soaking your foods in oil, you can enjoy the same crispy, delightful coating on the exterior, and a much lower fat count overall. Air fryers are definitely the best way to make your favourite foods healthier and more diet-friendly, so let's learn a bit more about them!

All About Air Fryers

If you don't yet own an air fryer but you're thinking of getting one (or if you do own one but you aren't quite sure how this amazing gadget works), it's best to think of an air fryer as a mini convection oven with superpowers. It isn't actually frying your food – what it does is closer to baking it, but the resulting taste and texture are very much like fried food.

Air fryers are known for being amazingly versatile, and they also cook quickly. They have seen an enormous uptake in recent years, and you can cook a whole range of foods in an air fryer, including frozen meat without needing to defrost it, and even things like cookies. Given how flexible they are, it's hardly surprising that so many people are keen to try these gadgets out.

To give a quick overview of just how versatile an air fryer is, the food categories you can cook in them include:

- Some baked goods

- Meat and fish

- Roasted vegetables

- Frozen finger foods

- Homemade finger foods

Almost anything can be made in an air fryer, although not absolutely everything can – so find a good recipe before you test this theory!

Simon C. Garfield

What Are The Pros Of Air Fryers?

There are a lot of advantages to using these cookers, but the biggest thing is the reduction in oil. It's thought that using an air fryer can often result in about a third of the oil use, depending on the approach and the food being cooked. If you are trying to cut back on oil, this is an amazing way to do it, without compromising on the taste and texture.

Another major advantage is the speed. Air fryers tend to cook food quickly, so you can have a finished meal on the table in a very short amount of time, which is ideal if you are feeding kids or working long hours (or both). They are also a great way to cook meat from frozen; if you have forgotten to thaw chicken or another meat before leaving the house for the day, you don't need to muck around with the microwave or cold water before cooking it. Air fryers get up to temperature fast enough to safely cook frozen meat.

Air fryers also tend to be reasonably cheap to buy, and will represent a major financial saving in oil if you regularly make fried foods. There are plenty of other reasons to use them, but these are the major advantages offered by this kind of cooker.

What Are The Cons Of Air Fryers?

Of course, no cooker is perfect, and an air fryer does have some drawbacks. One of the biggest is its capacity. Because they are counter-top machines, even a large air fryer can only make a relatively small amount of food at one time, and that means you have to cook food in batches. Because fried food needs to be eaten hot, this can be annoying, especially if you are feeding a lot of people. However, it is also often a problem when deep frying the traditional way, unless you have an industrial fryer, so it isn't a deal breaker in most cases.

Another issue with air fryers is that they do still use quite a bit of oil for food. It's massively reduced, but you can't cook without oil, so you will still be incorporating it into your diet regularly. It's also very easy to burn food in an air fryer, because of the high temperatures involved. You need to be hands-on and alert when cooking using this gadget, or it could ruin your dinner or even present a danger.

Air Fryer Use And Maintenance

If you've never used an air fryer before, it's important to point out that this is generally a very simple process. You will usually be brushing or spraying the food with oil, setting the temperature and time on your device, and then allowing the food to cook. This will usually take between 5 minutes and half an hour, depending on the foods you are making. Sometimes, you will need to turn the food halfway through, and at other times, you can just leave it to cook.

Simon C. Garfield

Of course, you need to maintain your air fryer if it is going to produce delicious foods for you; like all forms of cookers, it will need cleaning and caring for. Many people underestimate the maintenance involved when they first get an air fryer, and feel frustrated by this once they own one.

So, how do you look after your air fryer? Well, firstly, you need to let the whole thing cool down and then unplug it. Next, clean the basket, pan, and tray after every use, just as you would any cooking utensil. Some air fryers have dishwasher-safe components, while others will need to be hand-washed. In general, hand-washing is preferable because it will help these components to last longer.

Wash the utensils in hot, soapy water, using a soft cloth. If any bits of food are stuck on, soak the component for a while to loosen it and then have another go. Never use metal tools, wire wool, abrasive brushes, or any other tough scrubbers to get stuck residue off the components. This will scratch the non-stick coating and could permanently ruin that part of the equipment. Always be gentle when cleaning these parts.

You should also wipe out the inside of the air fryer with a damp, slightly soapy cloth to remove any residue. Be careful not to get the main part of the machine wet, however, because it is electric and this will destroy it. A damp cloth, followed by a thorough dry with a towel will be sufficient to keep the interior clean. Never put the main air fryer in the sink or the dishwasher.

What Is Air Fryer Food Like?

Air fryer food is actually closer to baked food in terms of how it is made, but it is very much like fried food, although slightly less greasy. Because of the coating of oil and the hot temperature, the food develops a deliciously crispy, satisfying coating on the outside, while remaining tender and succulent inside. Meat cooked in an air fryer will remain tender and chewy in the middle, but it will take on that deliciously crunchy exterior that is usually only found in deep fried foods.

That has made air fryer food enormously popular; it hits the craving for fat, retains the texture and juiciness of meat, and is better for you than normal fried food. It's ideal when you want something greasy and satisfying, but if you fancy something healthier, remember that you can also air fry vegetables. These will be akin to tender roasted vegetables, and they make an ideal side to a roast dinner.

Air fryer food is therefore a delicious option, and many people really enjoy eating it. However, if you aren't a fan of fried food overall, you will likely find that it's too greasy for you – even if the oil has been massively reduced compared with regular fried food!

Simon C. Garfield

What Common Mistakes Do People Make When Using An Air Fryer?

Before we start looking at some actual recipes, let's learn a bit about the commonest air fryer mistakes that people tend to make when they are using an air fryer. Understanding these in advance will help to ensure that you avoid them, meaning your food will taste better and your appliance will last longer!

- Don't put too much oil on your foods. Although many of us think of oil as adding that delicious taste and this might be a hard habit to break initially, putting a lot of oil on your foods will actually ruin them when you are using an air fryer. They will take on a greasy, heavy texture, and will turn limp rather than crispy. A light coating is often enough, and you can always add a second coating when you check on the food later if you decide it isn't getting enough crispiness.

- Don't forget to preheat your air fryer. Like getting the oil in the pan hot before you add your food, it's crucial to toss the food into a hot environment so that the outside crisps up immediately. Failure to do this will result in soggy food that just never takes on that mouth-watering crispy coating. Always preheat your air fryer; this shouldn't take long and makes an enormous difference to the meal.

- Take some time to learn which foods don't work well in an air fryer. When you get a shiny new kitchen gadget, it's always tempting to throw anything and everything into it to see what happens. Air fryers might be great, but they are not all-powerful. Foods need to be a certain weight in order to work in an air fryer, or they will simply get blown about by the fan, and won't cook properly. If you want to cook things like kale or tortillas in your air fryer, you'll need to weigh them down with other ingredients to stop them simply flying around in the basket.

- Always make sure you are using the right oil. It might not seem like it would make a difference, but remember that the oil's smoke point is important, especially when you are cooking at high temperatures (which air fryers always are). If you choose an oil with a low smoke point, such as coconut oil or canola oil, your food will burn. It will taste awful, and it's thought that the carcinogens that are created could be really bad for you.

  You should always be cooking with an oil that has a higher temperature than your cooking temperature. An air fryer's maximum temperature is usually around 480 degrees F, and that means it's crucial to choose an oil with a high smoke point, such as sunflower oil (486 degrees F), avocado oil (520 degrees F), peanut oil (440 degrees F), or sesame oil (450 degrees F). If you are cooking at a lower temperature, it may be okay to use a lower smoke point oil, but always check that your oil's smoke point is at least a few degrees higher than the hottest cooking temperature.

- Don't neglect to check on the food, either. Some cooking methods (e.g. ovens, slow cookers) lose a lot of heat when you open them to check on the food, so this tends to be discouraged. However, with air fryers, you can let this habit die, because they won't lose

Simon C. Garfield

notable amounts of heat when you take the food out, and air fried food often benefits from being turned, tossed, or re-oiled while it is cooking. Don't just set the timer and walk away.

- Don't overfill your air fryer's basket. It might be tempting if you are trying to cram enough food in there for your whole family to enjoy, but it simply will not work well. If the hot air cannot circulate around the food, it will not form a crispy coating. Instead, you will get uneven cooking, with some parts burning while other parts are still soft or even cold. Make sure you only fill the basket to its maximum quantity and allow air to circulate over all of the food. If this means cooking in batches, that's unfortunately your only option, because stuffing the basket will not work.

- Don't be afraid to experiment with new foods. Hopefully, this book is going to counteract this tendency anyway, but some people only use their air fryers for the standard fried foods, such as chips / fries, bacon, and chicken nuggets. However, an air fryer can make so many foods, it is absolutely worth using your air fryer to experiment and vary your diet. Don't limit yourself before you have even started!

- Remember to clean your air fryer regularly. We already touched on cleaning the air fryer after every use, but you should also do the occasional deep clean to remove any built-up residue. To achieve this, you will need to unplug and cool the air fryer, and then wipe it and clean it as mentioned above. Next, use a toothpick or a dedicated toothbrush (dry) to scrub out the insides and get into all the nooks and crannies. If crumbs of food build up in these areas, they will start to burn the next time you turn the fryer on, and this could ruin the taste of your new food, as well as creating an awful, acrid smell. Knock out the crumbs, and turn the air fryer over if necessary to get to all the different parts.

Make sure the air fryer is completely dry before you reassemble its parts. Never put wet components back into the machine, as this could be dangerous. Dry all the parts and allow any remaining moisture to air dry off them before putting everything back together.

If you follow these simple instructions, you should find that your air fryer cooking journey is smooth and straightforward! Keep your air fryer clean and keep experimenting with new recipes, and you'll find this gadget is a joy to have in your kitchen.

Simon C. Garfield

Great Air Fryer Recipes For Breakfast

An air fryer is often whipped out for making a tasty dinner, but what about breakfast? This meal is sometimes rushed and neglected, but it doesn't have to be. Your air fryer can make you amazing breakfast options on any day of the week, and it's a wonderfully quick, low-mess way to enjoy a fry-up.

Air Fried Hash Browns

Do you love hash browns? They are a great way to start the day, as potato is filling and contains plenty of nutrients. Fortunately, they are also super easy to make in an air fryer, and they are perfect for a weekend breakfast that the whole family can enjoy. You can make these with fresh potatoes, but surprisingly, frozen shredded potatoes will actually give you much crispier hash browns because they contain a lot less moisture! If you can use frozen, do.

SERVES: 4

You will need:

- 450 g / 16 oz shredded potatoes (preferably frozen)

- ½ teaspoon of garlic powder

- Salt and pepper to taste

Nutritional info:

Calories: 79

Fat: 0.1 g

Cholesterol: 0 mg

Sodium: 46 mg

Carbohydrates: 18.1 g

Fibre: 2.8 g

Protein: 2 g

Method:

1. Start by preheating your air fryer until it reaches 185 degrees C / 370 degrees F.

2. Open your bag of frozen potatoes (or shred your potatoes and drain as much liquid off them if you can if you don't have frozen potatoes) and weigh out the right amount. Tip this into your air fryer basket and then spray it with olive oil and sprinkle it with salt, pepper, and garlic powder. You can bump up the garlic powder if you like.

3. Cook the potatoes for about 18 or 19 minutes, checking on them occasionally. When they are starting to turn golden on top, use a wooden spatula to divide the portion up into four sections. Next, carefully flip them over.

4. Put them back into the air fryer and allow them to fry for another 5 minutes, or until they are as golden as you enjoy them.

5. Serve hot.

Simon C. Garfield

Air Fried Crispy Bacon And Eggs

Everybody loves bacon and eggs; they make the perfect breakfast treat, but it can be a pain to make in a pan. Bacon spits and hisses and splatters oil all over the place, so why not try making it in your air fryer? This is a brilliant way to enjoy your bacon and eggs, and it makes cooking so simple! You can even toss some toast in with it if you like, so the whole meal is made as one.

SERVES: 1

You will need:

- 2 eggs

- 2 strips of bacon

- 1 teaspoon of butter

- 2 slices of bread

Nutritional info:

Calories: 430

Fat: 30.2 g

Cholesterol: 424 mg

Sodium: 1167 mg

Carbohydrates: 10.4 g

Fibre: 0.4 g

Protein: 21.8 g

Method:

1. Take your slices of bread and lightly butter them. Put them in the air fryer basket with the butter facing down.

2. Cut your bacon slices in half. Take one slice per piece of bread, and curl the two halves to make a cup in the middle of the slice of bread. This will create a ring that holds the egg in the centre and prevents it from slipping down through the basket.

3. Crack the first egg onto the first piece of bread and the second onto the second piece of bread, inside the bacon rings you have created.

4. Place the basket inside the air fryer and cook it at 180 degrees C / 350 degrees F for around eight minutes, until the eggs have set and the bacon is crispy. Serve hot.

Simon C. Garfield

Asparagus And Egg Air Fryer Croquettes

If you love croquettes, these asparagus and egg ones will really hit the spot for you. They are a little more involved in terms of a breakfast meal, but well worth the extra work. However, be aware of the chilling time needed, and don't try to make these if you are rushing to get to work or starting a busy day, or you'll end up late.

SERVES: 6

You will need:

- 9 large eggs

- 25 g / ½ cup of spring onion / green onion

- 3 tablespoons of plain / all-purpose flour

- 3 tablespoons of butter

- 180 ml / ¾ cup of 2% milk

- 65 g / ½ cup of asparagus

- 75 g / 1/3 cup of cheese

- 210 g / 1 ¾ cups of breadcrumbs

- Salt and pepper to taste

- 1 tablespoon of tarragon

Nutritional info:

Calories: 335

Fat: 17.1 g

Cholesterol: 281 mg

Sodium: 520 mg

Carbohydrates: 29 g

Fibre: 2 g

Protein: 16.4 g

Simon C. Garfield

Method:

1. Hard boil 6 of the eggs and then plunge them into cold water and peel them.

2. Add your butter to a large saucepan and stir it over a medium heat until fully melted. Once it has melted, slowly sprinkle in the flour and stir until smooth, and then fry gently until it turns lightly golden.

3. Remove the pan from the heat and slowly add the milk, whisking well to prevent the flour from turning lumpy. Put it back over the heat and cook for a few more minutes, stirring occasionally, until the roux thickens into a white sauce.

4. Chop the hard boiled eggs into slices. Chop the onions and raw asparagus, shred the cheese, and mince the tarragon.

5. Stir these into your white sauce, along with salt and pepper to taste, and then transfer the mixture to a bowl and allow it to cool to room temperature. Once it has cooled, put it in the fridge for at least 2 hours.

6. When the mixture is ready, preheat your air fryer to 175 degrees C / 350 degrees F. Scoop your egg mixture into twelve equal portions and shape them into 3 inch long cylinders.

7. Tip your breadcrumbs into a bowl and roll the cylinders in them. Next, break your remaining three eggs into a separate bowl, and dip each cylinder in the egg wash and roll it in breadcrumbs again. This should ensure that each croquette has a good coating of crumbs. Pat more crumbs onto any spots that haven't got properly covered.

8. Grease your air fryer basket with cooking spray. Place a single layer of croquettes in the bottom of your air fryer basket and add a little more cooking spray. Cook for around 9 minutes, until they have turned golden brown all over. Turn them over, add a little more cooking spray if necessary, and then cook for another 3-5 minutes until fully gold all over. Serve hot and start the next batch.

Veg And Bacon Sweet Potato Skins

If you are looking for a more unusual breakfast, you might love these vegetable and bacon sweet potato skins. The air fryer makes the vegetables deliciously crispy and rich, and the sweet potato skins are a perfect start to the day, with a lovely earthy flavour. Cooked in the air fryer, the skins become crunchy and tempting. You can easily swap the sweet potatoes for yams if you prefer or if that's what you have available. You can also turn this recipe into a vegetarian option if you like by omitting the bacon or using a vegetarian or vegan substitute. Swap the whole milk for plant milk, and this can be a great vegan-friendly breakfast.

SERVES: 4

You will need:

- 1 small tomato
- 4 eggs
- 2 teaspoons of olive oil
- 2 sweet potatoes
- 4 slices of bacon
- 2 spring onions / green onions
- ½ red bell pepper
- Salt and pepper to taste
- 60 ml / ¼ cup of whole milk

Nutritional info:

Calories: 234

Fat: 13.6 g

Cholesterol: 182 ml

Sodium: 437 mg

Carbohydrates: 15.3 g

Fibre: 2.5 g

Protein: 13.2 g

Simon C. Garfield

Method:

1. Start by scrubbing your sweet potatoes and then make some slits in their skins, across the length. Place them in the microwave for about 7 minutes. You want them to be soft, so microwave them for longer if necessary.

2. While the potatoes are microwaving, cook the bacon and chop up the tomato, onion, and red pepper.

3. Slice the potatoes lengthwise (use a towel to protect your hands as the potatoes will be very hot and may release a lot of steam). Scoop the flesh out, leaving a little around the edges, and set the flesh aside. You won't be using it in this recipe but it can be used to create sweet potato and carrot mash, or for other purposes.

4. Brush the potato skins with olive oil and a little salt, and then put them in your air fryer basket and cook them for 10 minutes at 400 degrees F.

5. Get a non-stick skillet and warm it over a low-medium heat, and then add the milk, eggs, pepper, and salt. Stir gently and keep cooking until the egg has turned completely firm.

6. Take the potato skins out of the air fryer and add ¼ of your mixture, plus some crumbled bacon, to each skin. Put the skin back into the air fryer and cook for another 3 minutes. If you want to add some cheese to this recipe, you can melt it onto the skins at this point.

7. Once cooked, sprinkle your chopped onions, tomatoes, and red pepper across them and serve hot.

Simon C. Garfield

Air Fried Cinnamon Toast

Do you love eating crispy cinnamon toast first thing? This is a great, simple recipe you can whip up in no time in your air fryer. It's perfect if you'd rather have a basic breakfast that's ready in minutes.

SERVES: 2

You will need:

- 1 tablespoon of sugar

- 3 tablespoons of butter

- 4 slices of bread

- ½ teaspoon of cinnamon (or more to taste)

Nutritional info:

Calories: 155

Fat: 9.5 g

Cholesterol: 23 mg

Sodium: 232 mg

Carbohydrates: 15.9 g

Fibre: 0.8 g

Protein: 2 g

Method:

1. Preheat your air fryer to 200 degrees C / 400 degrees F.

2. Get a small bowl and stir together the soft butter with the cinnamon and some sugar. You can adjust the quantities to match your preferences. Mix it well so the spice and sugar is well distributed.

3. Butter your bread, spreading the butter right to the corners of the slices. Be generous so you get plenty of flavouring.

4. Place the slices of bread in the air fryer basket, with the buttered side facing up, and cook for 5 minutes.

5. Serve with fresh fruit and a little more cinnamon, or a pinch of nutmeg if you prefer.

Simon C. Garfield

Baked Apples In An Air Fryer

Do you love baked apples? Get a bit of fruit into your diet to start the day with this rich and creamy recipe. Kids will love it too!

SERVES: 4

You will need:

- 2 apples

- 3 teaspoons of honey

- ½ teaspoon of ground cinnamon

- 45 g / ½ cup of oats

- 2 tablespoons of butter

Nutritional info:

Calories: 164

Fat: 6.6 g

Cholesterol: 15 mg

Sodium: 43 mg

Carbohydrates: 26.9 g

Fibre: 3.9 g

Protein: 1.7 g

Method:

1. Preheat your air fryer to 180 degrees C / 375 degrees F.

2. Melt your butter in a small bowl, and then cut and core your apples. Brush the butter across each half.

3. In a separate bowl, mix the remaining butter with the oats, cinnamon, and honey.

4. Place the apples in your air fryer basket, buttery side up, and spoon the mixture on top of the halves.

5. Put the apples in the air fryer and cook them for up to 15 minutes, until they have turned rich and golden.

6. Top them with some ice cream or whipped cream and serve sizzling hot.

Simon C. Garfield

Air Fryer Frittatas

Do you love frittatas? They make a quick and ultra simple breakfast, and the great news is that you can add anything you like to them to make them shine. No matter what ingredients you enjoy, these can be adapted to suit it, and they will be loved by everyone in the family. They are pretty quick and easy, and can be made in under an hour.

SERVES: 2

You will need:

- 4 large eggs

- 2 tablespoons of diced red bell pepper

- 1 green onion

- 60 g / ½ cup of cheddar

- 115 g / ¼ lb of breakfast sausage

- Pinch of cayenne pepper

Nutritional info:

Calories: 475

Fat: 34.8 g

Cholesterol: 405 mg

Sodium: 728 mg

Carbohydrates: 10.7 g

Fibre: 1.8 g

Protein: 30.5 g

Method:

1. Start by cooking your sausages until they are completely done, and then allow them to cool a little and crumble them. Chop up the green onion and grate the cheddar cheese.

2. Preheat your air fryer to 180 degrees C / 360 degrees F.

3. Get out a large mixing bowl and add your bell pepper, cayenne pepper, onion, sausage, and eggs to it. Mix them thoroughly until they are completely combined.

4. Spray a non-stick cake tin with oil and tip the egg mixture into the tin. Place it in your air fryer and cook it until the egg sets. This should take about twenty minutes.

Superb Air Fryer Dinners

Your air fryer will really come into its own when dinner time rolls around. The best thing about this gadget is its speed; you won't find yourself waiting for hours for your oven to heat and the food to slowly, slowly cook while you just want to kick back and relax at the end of a long day. Your air fryer is super speedy and will mean you can have dinner on the table in less than an hour.

Air Fryer Chicken Breast

Your air fryer is a brilliant way to make chicken breast, because it's super fast and simple – much quicker than in the oven. You just season the chicken breasts, toss them in the basket, and fry them until they are thoroughly sizzling and delicious. This is a brilliant way to get juicy, tender chicken breasts with minimal work.

SERVES: 4

You will need:

- 4 boneless chicken breasts with the skins removed
- ½ teaspoon of garlic powder
- ½ teaspoon of salt
- ½ teaspoon of dried oregano
- Cooking spray
- Pinch of pepper

Simon C. Garfield

Nutritional info:

Calories: 203

Fat: 4.5 g

Cholesterol: 112 mg

Sodium: 380 mg

Carbohydrates: 0.4 g

Fibre: 0.1 g

Protein: 37.2 g

Method:

1. Preheat your air fryer to 180 degrees C / 360 degrees F.

2. Take out a small mixing bowl and stir together the garlic powder, oregano, salt, and pepper.

3. Spray the chicken breasts on the smooth side with avocado oil.

4. Sprinkle the seasoning over the chicken breasts and then put the chicken breasts in the air fryer with the seasoned side facing down.

5. Spray oil on the side facing up and add a little more seasoning.

6. Cook the chicken breasts for about 10 minutes, until they are starting to brown. Flip them over and cook them for another 10 minutes. Use a meat thermometer to check that the internal temperature has reached at least 73 degrees C / 165 degrees F, and keep cooking them if the inside of the meat is not yet this hot. It must meet this temperature to be safe to consume.

7. When the chicken is hot through, take it out of the air fryer and set it on a plate to rest for around 5 minutes. This gives the juices time to redistribute through the meat and prevents them from being lost when you cut the chicken open.

French Fries In Your Air Fryer

If you love crispy chips / fries, an air fryer is the way to go. This is the best way to get chips / fries that are golden and crunchy on the outside and delightfully soft and puffy in the centre. Forget chip pans with dangerous amounts of hot oil and the potential for setting your kitchen on fire – your air fryer is the way to go. Air fried chips / fries are also far healthier than any other kind, and you can get them just the way you like them.

SERVES: 6

You will need:

- 3 big potatoes
- Salt and pepper to taste
- 2 tablespoons of olive oil

Nutritional info:

Calories: 114

Fat: 4.8 g

Cholesterol: 0 mg

Sodium: 34 mg

Carbohydrates: 16.7 g

Fibre: 2.6 g

Protein: 1.8 g

Simon C. Garfield

Method:

1. Wash and scrub your potatoes, and peel them if you would rather not eat the skins (although the skins can turn deliciously crispy in the fryer, so this isn't a necessity).

2. Chop the potatoes into long, thin strips. You can go as fat or as thin as you prefer, but traditional French fries are thin strips of potato, rather than big wedges, and these tend to cook better and faster in the air fryer.

3. Get a bath of cold water and submerge your potato chunks in the water so that they are completely covered. Leave them to soak for one hour. This removes excess starch from the water and ensures that your fries will turn crispy and delicious in the air fryer.

4. When your fries are nearly ready, preheat your air fryer to 190 degrees C / 375 degrees F.

5. Drain the fries and pat the excess water off them, and then toss them with oil, salt, and pepper.

6. Put the fries in a single layer in the bottom of the fryer basket and then put the basket in the air fryer and cook the fries for about 10 minutes. Give them a gentle toss, and cook for a further 3 minutes, until they are golden and crispy.

7. If you need to do more than one batch of fries, put the finished fries on a baking sheet in a warm oven and leave them to rest while you cook the other fries. This will make it easier to get everything piping hot when you serve the meal.

Simon C. Garfield

Avocado And Bacon Fries

Do you love avocado? If so, it's well worth trying these amazing avocado and bacon fries, which are quick and simple to make, and are the perfect way to enjoy avocado. They aren't the healthiest thing on the planet, with all that bacon, but they are absolutely delicious. The recipe makes 24, so there's enough for everyone to have two, or one if you're serving up at a party. These are an appetizer that's bound to wow your guests, and they are very easy to make!

SERVES: 12

You will need:

- 24 strips of bacon
- 3 avocados

Nutritional info:

Calories: 308

Fat: 25.7 g

Cholesterol: 42 mg

Sodium: 881 mg

Carbohydrates: 4.9 g

Fibre: 3.4 g

Protein: 15 g

Simon C. Garfield

Method:

1. Preheat your air fryer to 200 degrees C / 400 degrees F.

2. Scoop the avocado flesh out of the skins and slice each one into eight wedges. Remove the pits as you work; you should get four slices from each half of the fruit. Try to get them close in size, as this will ensure even cooking.

3. Wrap each piece in bacon, trimming the bacon if necessary, and then arrange them in a single layer in the bottom of your air fryer basket. Put the bacon's seam down, as this will help it all to stay together in the fryer. You will need to make multiple batches.

4. Cook them for around 8 minutes, until the bacon is fully cooked and starting to turn crispy. Serve them hot with any dipping sauce you fancy.

Air Fryer Crispy Salmon

If you love salmon, you might be delighted to learn that you can cook it very easily in your air fryer. This will give you crispy, flaky fish full of delicious and rich juices. Serve with some lemon and cream cheese for the perfect recipe, and enjoy that crispy crust you won't get with any other cooking method. It's a good idea to leave the skin on your salmon, because this will help to trap the juices in while it cooks.

SERVES: 2

You will need:

- 2 tablespoons of butter

- 1 sliced lemon

- 1 teaspoon of garlic salt

- 1 teaspoon of chopped parsley

- 450 g / 1 lb of salmon fillets

Nutritional info:

Calories: 411

Fat: 25.6

Cholesterol: 131 mg

Sodium: 183 mg

Carbohydrates: 2.8 g

Fibre: 0.8 g

Protein: 44.5 g

Method:

1. Preheat your air fryer to 200 degrees C / 400 degrees F.

2. Season your salmon fillets with the garlic salt, rubbing it into the flesh.

3. Put the salmon in the air fryer basket in a single layer, with the skin side facing down.

4. Brush butter onto the salmon and top it with lemon slices (add more if you like lemony salmon, and fewer if you prefer a less sour flavour).

5. Fry the salmon for up to 13 minutes (depending on how thick it is) and then check whether it has reached an internal temperature of 62 degrees C / 145 degrees F.

6. Serve hot with a side of peas, potatoes, cream cheese, or on a bed of rice.

Fried Broccoli

Do you prefer a bit of a healthier approach? If you want deliciously crispy broccoli for the side to another meal, your air fryer can supply it. This goes wonderfully with seafood or rice dishes.

SERVES: 4

You will need:

- 1 medium broccoli head
- 1 clove of garlic
- 1 tablespoon of olive oil
- Pinch of red pepper flakes
- Pinch of black pepper
- Pinch of salt

Nutritional info:

Calories: 53

Fat: 3.7 g

Cholesterol: 0 mg

Sodium: 60 mg

Carbohydrates: 4.5 g

Fibre: 1.7 g

Protein: 1.9 g

Method:

1. Wash and chop the broccoli and shake it dry.

2. Mince your garlic and preheat your air fryer to 190 degrees C / 370 degrees F.

3. Mix the broccoli, oil, and garlic, and stir in some red pepper flakes.

4. Add a single layer of the broccoli to the air fryer basket, and then cook it for 10 minutes until it turns soft and delicious. The outside should take on a slight crispiness, and then the broccoli is ready to serve. You may need to make multiple batches, depending on the size of your air fryer.

Simon C. Garfield

Lemon And Pepper Air Fried Shrimp

If you love seafood, you can make an amazing air fried shrimp with lemon and pepper, and it's perfect for a fancy date night or a luxury birthday dinner. These shrimps go really well tossed through spaghetti, but you can also serve them with salad, new potatoes, or rice – the choice is yours. This dish is super flexible and delicious, and takes very little time to make.

SERVES: 4

You will need:

- 2 tablespoons of lemon juice

- 120 ml / ½ cup of olive oil

- 450 g / 1 lb of raw shrimp (weighed after peeling and deveining)

- ½ teaspoon of salt

- 1 teaspoon of pepper

Nutritional info:

Calories: 354

Fat: 27.2 g

Cholesterol: 239 mg

Sodium: 569 mg

Carbohydrates: 2.2 g

Fibre: 0.2 g

Protein: 26 g

Simon C. Garfield

Method:

1. Preheat the air fryer to 200 degrees C / 400 degrees F.

2. Peel, devein, and clean the raw shrimps, and discard the waste.

3. Cut your lemon in half and squeeze out 2 tablespoons of lemon juice.

4. Get out a medium bowl and add the lemon juice, olive oil, pepper, and salt. Whisk well.

5. Drop the shrimps in the bowl and turn them back and forth to combine them with the juice. Allow them to stand for a few minutes.

6. Line your air fryer basket with parchment paper to prevent the juice from dripping through, and then take the shrimps out of the juice and drop them into the air fryer. Cook for 4 minutes and then give the shrimps a good shake and cook for another 4 minutes. They should turn white and opaque, with a little browning, when they are fully cooked.

7. Take them out of the air fryer and stir them through pasta (or an alternative dish) with the remaining lemony sauce drizzled across the top.

Chicken Fajitas

If you love tortillas and chicken, this recipe is the one for you. It's super simple, but it also packs in some vegetables, and you can adapt it to suit your tastes with ease. The air fryer will make all the ingredients deliciously crispy and succulent, and this meal can hit the table in around 30 minutes – making it perfect for a busy week night meal. Don't be afraid to play around with the spices if you find the flavour too strong, or add a little sour cream or cream cheese to mellow them out.

SERVES: 4

You will need:

- 1 large red or yellow bell pepper

- ½ pound of boneless, skinless chicken breasts

- 1 red onion

- 1 tablespoon of chilli powder (reduce this if you don't enjoy spicy food)

- 1 teaspoon of cumin

- 1 tablespoon of corn oil

- 2 teaspoons of lemon juice (or lime juice)

- Salt and pepper to taste

- 4 tortillas

Nutritional info:

Calories: 219

Fat: 8.9 g

Cholesterol: 50 mg

Sodium: 82 mg

Carbohydrates: 16.9 g

Fibre: 3.2 g

Protein: 18.7 g

Method:

1. Preheat your air fryer to 185 degrees C / 370 degrees F.

2. Wash the pepper and cut it into thin strips. Peel your onion and cut it into strips too.

3. Cut the chicken into ½ inch strips.

4. Get out a large mixing bowl and add the corn oil, lemon juice, chilli powder, cumin, chicken strips, onion, bell pepper, salt, and pepper, and mix thoroughly. Allow it to sit for a few minutes to let the flavours combine.

5. Transfer the ingredients to your air fryer basket and cook for 6 minutes, and then take the basket out and shake the contents around. Cook for another 6 minutes, until crispy and delicious.

6. Use a meat thermometer to check that the chicken has reached an internal temperature of at least 165 degrees F.

7. Warm the tortillas and top them with your fajita mix, and then enjoy with any fresh herbs or spices you like.

Air Fried Sweet And Sour Chicken

If sweet and sour chicken is a top favourite for you, you might be delighted to learn that you can make it yourself in your air fryer with just a few fairly common ingredients. Amazingly, this is another recipe that you can have on the table in under an hour. You can serve it with rice or with pitta breads, or anything else you fancy. Do note that unless you add food colouring, this won't achieve the classic red-orange glow of takeaway sweet and sour sauce, but it will be just as delicious.

SERVES: 2

For the sweet and sour sauce, you will need:

- 235 ml / 1 cup of pineapple juice

- 1 tablespoon of soy sauce

- 100 g brown / ½ cup of brown sugar

- 3 tablespoons of rice wine vinegar

- 2 tablespoons of cornflour / cornstarch

- 2 tablespoons of water

- ½ teaspoon of ground ginger

To make the chicken, you will also need:

- 2 tablespoons of cornflour / cornstarch

- 450 g / 1 pound of chicken breasts

Some people like to serve this with some additional pineapple chunks mixed through the sauce, but this is optional (not included in nutritional information).

Simon C. Garfield

Nutritional info:

Calories: 712

Fat: 17.3 g

Cholesterol: 202 mg

Sodium: 660 mg

Carbohydrates: 65.3 g

Fibre: 0.9 g

Protein: 67.2 g

Method:

1. Preheat your air fryer to 200 degrees C / 400 degrees F.

2. Cut your chicken pieces into around 2 inch chunks.

3. Mix 2 tablespoons of cornflour / cornstarch and chicken pieces together in a bowl and make sure the chicken is fully coated.

4. Add the chicken to your air fryer basket and cook for about 5 minutes. Take it out and shake the basket, and then cook for another 4 minutes.

5. In a pan, mix together your brown sugar, rice wine vinegar, soy sauce, ginger, and pineapple juice. Bring this to a simmer, stirring gently.

6. In a bowl, mix the remaining 2 tablespoons of cornflour / cornstarch with the water to create a gloopy mixture, and then tip it into the sweet and sour sauce. If you are adding extra pineapple chunks, tip them in too. Stir well and allow to simmer for another minute.

7. Toss the chicken into the sauce and stir well, and then serve over rice or noodles.

Air Fried Baked Potatoes

Baked potatoes are a fantastic meal and can be paired with any topping, but if you want to make them in the oven, they take a long time. You need to think about your meal in advance in order to put potatoes on, as big ones can take over an hour to cook in the oven. Microwaving them is quicker, but you don't get the delightfully crispy skins – so why not get your air fryer to help out again?

Baked potatoes are a healthy meal and the great news is, you can have them with any toppings you fancy – salads, sour cream, chopped vegetables, baked beans, cheese, chilli, tuna, and more. No matter what you love, baked potatoes are a perfect base.

SERVES: 4

You will need:

- 4 large potatoes

- 1 tablespoon of olive oil

- ½ teaspoon of salt

Nutritional info:

Calories: 285

Fat: 3.9 g

Cholesterol: 0 mg

Sodium: 313 mg

Carbohydrates: 58 g

Fibre: 8.9 g

Protein: 6.2 g

Simon C. Garfield

Method:

1. Preheat your air fryer to 200 degrees C / 400 degrees F.

2. Take out your potatoes and scrub them with running water. Don't remove the skins; these will turn crispy and delicious in the air fryer.

3. Dry the potatoes thoroughly and stab them with a fork in various places. This will let the steam vent out of them so they don't explode in the air fryer.

4. Rub the potatoes with salt and oil, and then put them in the air fryer basket and cook them for 30 minutes. Take them out, flip them over, and squeeze gently (using a towel) to see if they are nearly done. If they are starting to turn tender, they should take between 5 and 10 more minutes. If they are still hard, give them 15 minutes longer. The bigger the potato, the longer it needs to stay in the air fryer for.

5. When they are soft, use tongs to lift the potatoes out and place them on a plate. Add whatever toppings you prefer, and enjoy hot.

Steak And Mushroom Bites

If you are prepared to put in a little more time to make a truly special meal, these air fried steak and mushroom bites are delicious. They do take a little over an hour to make because the meat needs to marinate, but they are perfect for a fancy meal, or used to top rice. Roast some root vegetables to go with it as another option. You can make your steak as rare as you want for this recipe, so keep an eye on your air fryer and the colour of the meat as you work.

SERVES: 2

Simon C. Garfield

You will need:

- 450 g / 1 lb Sirloin steak

- 2 tablespoons of avocado oil

- ½ teaspoon of garlic powder

- 1 teaspoon of kosher salt

- ¼ of black peppercorn

- 250 g / 8 oz mushrooms

- 2 tablespoons of Worcestershire sauce

Nutritional info:

Calories: 482

Fat: 16.3 g

Cholesterol: 203 mg

Sodium: 1484 mg

Carbohydrates: 8.2 g

Fibre: 1.9 g

Protein: 72.7 g

Method:

1. Cut your steak into 1.5 inch cubes and wash and slice the mushrooms.

2. Get a large bowl and add all of the ingredients. Toss the meat to coat it in the sauce, and then place it in the fridge to marinate for one hour.

3. Preheat your air fryer to 200 degrees C / 400 degrees F. Spray the inside of the cooker basket with oil and then lift the steak and mushrooms out of the marinade and add them to the basket.

4. Fry for 5 minutes, and then shake the ingredients. Cook for another 5 minutes.

5. Use a meat thermometer to check whether the insides of the meat have reached the temperature you desire (see the guide below).

6. Serve hot and sizzling.

Steak temperature guide:

For rare steak: 51 degrees C / 125 degrees F

For medium-rare: 55 degrees C / 130 degrees F

For medium: 60 degrees C / 140 degrees F

For medium-well: 65 degrees C / 150 degrees F

For well done: 71 degrees C / 160 degrees F

Macaroni Cheese

If mac and cheese is a favourite recipe in your household, you will be delighted to learn that this can also be made in an air fryer with very little extra work. In less than an hour, you can have a delicious, sizzling, crispy mac and cheese on the table, ready for the hungry family to devour. This classic dish is loved by everyone, and it couldn't be easier to make in an air fryer – although you should note that you will need an air fryer handled pan for it.

SERVES: 5

You will need:

- 480 ml / 2 cups of whole milk
- 4 tablespoons of butter
- 240 ml / 1 cup of vegetable stock
- 4 tablespoons of cream cheese
- 230 g / 8 oz cheddar cheese
- 230 g / 8 oz dry pasta (macaroni is best but any short pasta will work)
- 120 g / 1 cup of mozzarella
- ¼ teaspoon white pepper
- ¼ teaspoon of salt
- 1 teaspoon of mustard
- Pinch of cayenne pepper
- Pinch of nutmeg

Nutritional info:

Calories: 503

Fat: 32.6 g

Cholesterol: 127 mg

Sodium: 725 mg

Carbohydrates: 30.8 g

Fibre: 0.2 g

Protein: 22.2 g

Simon C. Garfield

Method:

1. Preheat your air fryer to 200 degrees C / 400 degrees F.

2. Rinse the pasta with hot water and then drain it.

3. Get a large, microwave-safe bowl and add the butter, cream cheese, milk, and stock to it. Microwave in short bursts until the butter has melted and stir well. You don't need to get it boiling, so it should only take about 3 minutes.

4. Grate the cheddar.

5. Get a large bowl and mix together the mozzarella, pasta, cheddar, nutmeg, cayenne pepper, salt, pepper, and the melted stock mixture.

6. Pour this mixture into an air fryer handled pan, and then place some greased parchment paper across the top, followed by a layer of tinfoil. Put the pan into the air fryer and cook it for 35 minutes.

7. Use a fork to check whether the pasta is done, cooking for up to 10 more minutes if not. Remove the lids when complete, stir, and serve hot.

EXCLUSIVE BONUS

40 Weight Loss Recipes

&

14 Days Meal Plan

Scan the QR-Code and receive
the FREE download:

Bonus – Lunchtime Inspirations

An air fryer isn't a great option if you're not at home to use it for your lunches, because fried food isn't nice when left to go cold. That might mean you rarely get to use your air fryer to make lunch (unless you work from home). When you do have the opportunity, however, it's a fantastic way to enjoy a quick, easy, and satisfying lunch – so let's look at some great lunchtime ideas you can try!

Air Fried Pizza

Do you love pizza for lunch? Air fryer pizza is fantastic and shouldn't take you long to make – so be prepared to enjoy some stringy, cheesy goodness. Again, this recipe can easily be adapted to include all your favourite toppings, so feel free to adjust it however you like. It's a super simple and fun way to enjoy pizza on your lunch break.

SERVES: 1

You will need:

- 2 tablespoons of tomato sauce
- ¼ cup of mozzarella cheese (or substitute half of this for cheddar if you choose)
- 1 whole wheat pitta bread
- 8 slices of pepperoni
- 1 tablespoon of chopped parsley to serve (or other herbs if you prefer)
- Cooking spray

Nutritional info:

Calories: 421

Fat: 22.9 g

Cholesterol: 50 mg

Sodium: 1273 mg

Carbohydrates: 37.3 g

Fibre: 5.3 g

Protein: 18.8 g

Method:

1. Take your pitta and spread your tomato sauce across the top of it. Leave a small border around the edges; this will crisp up while it cooks.

2. Grate your mozzarella or cheddar and then sprinkle this across the top, along with the pepperoni slices.

3. Lightly spray the top of your pizza with cooking oil and place it in the bottom of the air fryer basket. Cook at 200 degrees C / 400 degrees F for around 6 minutes and then check on it. It may need another couple of minutes. The cheese should be fully melted and gooey by the time you serve it.

4. Lift it out of the air fryer basket using a spatula and allow it to cool slightly, and then slice and serve.

Vegetable And Ham Omelette

If you love simple lunches and you're in a bit of a hurry, did you know that you can make a delicious, nutritious, and simple omelette in your air fryer? The beauty of this recipe is that you can add any vegetables you enjoy, plus cheese, spices, herbs, and anything else you like. This is one of the most versatile recipes out there, and it takes less than 10 minutes to make!

SERVES: 1

You will need:

- 50 g / 1.7 oz of ham

- 50 g / 1.7 oz of mushrooms

- ½ red bell pepper

- 1 green onion

- 60 ml / ¼ cup of milk

- 2 eggs

- 55 g / ¼ cup of mozzarella

- Pinch of salt

- Herbs of your choice

Nutritional info:

Calories: 292

Fat: 15.9 g

Cholesterol: 365 mg

Sodium: 1008 mg

Carbohydrates: 13.1 g

Fibre: 2.3 g

Protein: 25.8 g

Method:

1. Get out a small bowl and crack the eggs into it. Add the milk and whisk thoroughly until frothy.

2. Wash and chop the vegetables into fine slices, and then add them to the egg mix, along with a pinch of salt.

3. Grease a 3 inch x 6 inch pan and pour the egg mixture into it.

4. Place the pan in the basket of the air fryer and cook at 175 degrees C / 350 degrees F for 4 minutes.

5. Toss the cheese in and cook for a further 4-6 minutes, until the eggs have solidified to your liking.

6. Lift the basket out and use a rubber spatula to gently ease the edges of the egg away from the pan. Slip the spatula underneath the edge and serve with additional toppings.

Simon C. Garfield

Air Fried Chicken, Veg, And Rice

If you're feeling some fried rice for lunch, this is extremely easy to create in your air fryer. It should only take a few minutes to throw together the necessary ingredients, and you can easily make this vegetarian or even vegan by omitting the chicken. All the ingredients are things you are likely to have at home, and it's easy to make a large portion of this rice to enjoy throughout the week! Note that you will again need a suitable pan for this recipe; the rice will go through the holes in the air fryer basket otherwise.

SERVES: 8

You will need:

- 25 g / ½ cup of onion

- 140 g / 1 cup of chicken

- 525 g / 3 cups of cooked white rice

- 1 tablespoon of vegetable oil

- 140 g / 1 cup of peas

- 150 g / 1 cup of carrots

- 6 tablespoons of soy sauce

Nutritional info:

Calories: 325

Fat: 2.8 g

Cholesterol: 13 mg

Sodium: 715 mg

Carbohydrates: 61.3 g

Fibre: 2.6 g

Protein: 12 g

Simon C. Garfield

Method:

1. Cook some white rice until done, and then rinse it with cold water and set it aside to cool.

2. Dice your chicken and cook it, and peel and chop the onion.

3. Get a large mixing bowl and add the cold rice to it. Pour in the vegetable oil and the soy sauce, and mix well.

4. Add the onion, peas, carrots, chicken, and onion, and mix well.

5. Pour the rice into a lightly greased pan, and put it in your air fryer at 180 degrees C / 350 degrees F for 20 minutes. You may wish to take it out and shake it occasionally, but it should need minimal attention.

6. Serve hot and enjoy! Store any leftovers in the fridge or the freezer once they have reached room temperature.

Garlicky Brussels Sprouts

Are you on a bit of a health kick and looking for some way to make your lunch better without having to make too many sacrifices? These amazing Brussels sprouts are the answer, and you can eat them as they are for an ultra-healthy lunch option, or toss them into a salad or put them together with a pitta bread. No matter how you eat them, these sweet, garlicky, nutty treats will not disappoint!

SERVES: 4

Simon C. Garfield

You will need:

- 3 cloves of garlic

- ¼ teaspoon of pepper

- ½ teaspoon of salt

- 3 tablespoons of olive oil

- 450 g / 1 lb of Brussels sprouts

- 1 ½ teaspoon of fresh rosemary

- 50 g / ½ cup of breadcrumbs

Nutritional info:

Calories: 197

Fat: 11.7 g

Cholesterol: 0 mg

Sodium: 419 mg

Carbohydrates: 21.1 g

Fibre: 5.1 g

Protein: 5.8 g

Method:

1. Preheat your air fryer to 175 degrees C / 350 degrees F.

2. Wash and trim your Brussels sprouts, and cut them into halves.

3. Mince the garlic and put it in a small, microwave-safe bowl. Add the salt, pepper, and olive oil and microwave it on high for 30 seconds.

4. Toss the Brussels sprouts into the mixture and stir, and then lift out and add to a tray inside your air fryer basket. Cook for about 4 minutes, and then stir and cook again for another 4 minutes. Stir once more and cook for another 4 minutes. The sprouts should then be turning brown and tender.

5. Mince the rosemary and toss it with the breadcrumbs, and then add the leftover oil and garlic mixture. Sprinkle this across the sprouts and cook for another 3-4 minutes, until truly tender and delicious. Serve hot and enjoy.

Air Fried Asparagus

Following on from the healthy Brussels sprouts, if you're an asparagus-lover, you can also make this delicious vegetable in your air fryer quickly and easily. This makes a fabulous lunch to throw together, and you can serve it with cheese, a side of rice, new potatoes, or stirred through pasta – or just have it plain! This vegetable is good enough to enjoy on its own, especially when crispy and hot.

SERVES: 4

You will need:

- 450 g / 1 lb of asparagus
- 4 teaspoons of olive oil
- ½ teaspoon of pepper
- 1 clove of garlic
- 55 g / ¼ cup of mayonnaise
- 28 g Parmesan
- 1 ½ teaspoons of lemon zest
- ¼ teaspoon of salt

Nutritional info:

Calories: 145

Fat: 11.2 g

Cholesterol: 9 mg

Sodium: 267 mg

Carbohydrates: 8.7 g

Fibre: 2.5 g

Protein: 5 g

Simon C. Garfield

Method:

1. Preheat your air fryer to 190 degrees C / 375 degrees F.

2. Wash your asparagus and trim the ends off. Mince your garlic and add this, the asparagus, the olive oil, the mayonnaise, the lemon zest, the pepper, and the salt to a large bowl. Toss everything together until the asparagus is thoroughly coated.

3. Place a single layer of asparagus on a greased tray at the bottom of your air fryer basket and cook for about 5 minutes, until tender and brown. You will likely need to work in batches. When you have cooked all of the asparagus, transfer it to a platter and sprinkle the grated Parmesan across it.

Fried Aubergine / Eggplant Circles

Do you love aubergine / eggplant? This vegetable has been making waves lately, and many people love its velvety, delicious texture, and the silky response it has to being coated in oils. If you haven't got time to whip up a moussaka, you can still enjoy aubergine, but instead, it will become crispy and delicious from your air fryer.

SERVES: 6

You will need:

- 240 g / 2 cups of breadcrumbs

- 70 g / ½ cup of plain / all-purpose flour

- 1 egg

- 1 medium aubergine / eggplant

- ¼ teaspoon of pepper

- Pinch of salt

- 1 ½ tablespoons of Italian seasoning

- Cooking spray

Nutritional info:

Calories: 221

Fat: 4 g

Cholesterol: 30 mg

Sodium: 327 mg

Carbohydrates: 38.9 g

Fibre: 4.6 g

Protein: 7.6 g

Method:

1. Get out a shallow bowl and break the egg into it. Whisk well. In a second bowl, measure out your flour, and in a third, measure the breadcrumbs.

2. Preheat your air fryer to 190 degrees C / 380 degrees F.

3. Wash your aubergine / eggplant and slice the end off it. Cut it into ¼ inch circles and place these on a plate.

4. Dip each one first into the flour, then into the egg, then into the breadcrumbs. Make sure that both sides get covered in breadcrumbs, as this will make the slices crispy and delicious.

5. Lay the aubergine / eggplant slices in the bottom of your air fryer basket with no overlap and cook for 8 minutes. Take them out, flip them over, spray the tops with a little oil, and cook for another 3 minutes, until the breadcrumbs are crispy and golden. Serve immediately with a creamy dip or spicy sauce.

Crispy Turkey Croquettes

If you love the crunchiness of breadcrumbs and you're a fan of turkey meat, these crispy turkey croquettes are ideal for your lunches. They are a great way to use up leftovers after Thanksgiving, but they're also a meal in their own right, and you can easily freeze them. The recipe makes enough for 6, but if you want all your lunches for the week sorted in advance, simply toss some of these in the freezer with greaseproof paper between each one, and then get out individual portions and serve hot with baked beans or rice. Kids are bound to love these too!

Note that if you aren't a turkey fan, you can make these croquettes with pretty much any kind of meat, or even fish. Simply swap the meat for the one of your preference, and consider altering the herbs if something might match better (e.g. dill if you are cooking fish). This is a great way to make this recipe even more versatile and suit various different tastes in the family.

SERVES: 6

You will need:

- 45 g / ½ cup of Parmesan

- 45 g / ½ cup of Swiss cheese

- 150 g / 1 ¼ cups of breadcrumbs

- 725 g / 4 cups of cooked turkey

- 1 egg

- 420 g / 2 cups of mashed potatoes (including milk and a little butter for creaminess)

- ½ teaspoon of salt

- ¼ teaspoon of pepper

- Cooking spray

- 1 shallot

- 1 teaspoon of fresh sage

- 2 teaspoons of fresh rosemary

- 2 tablespoons of water

Nutritional info:

Calories: 362

Fat: 12.3 g

Cholesterol: 103 mg

Sodium: 664 mg

Carbohydrates: 30.7 g

Fibre: 1 g

Protein: 31.4 g

Method:

1. Preheat your air fryer to 175 degrees C / 350 degrees F.

2. Grate your cheese and mince the rosemary and sage.

3. Take out a large bowl and add the mashed potatoes, grated cheeses, minced herbs, along with the salt and the pepper.

4. Cook and chop your turkey, and stir this into the bowl until thoroughly combined.

5. Use your hands to shape the mixture into patties (you should get about 12, around one inch thick).

6. Take a clean bowl and whisk together the egg and water. Put the breadcrumbs in a second bowl.

7. Dip each croquette into the egg mixture and then roll it in the breadcrumbs. Pat the coating down well to make the breadcrumbs stick, and then grease a tray and place it inside your air fryer basket. Add the turkey croquettes in a single layer and spritz lightly with some cooking spray.

8. Cook for about 5 minutes, and then flip and spritz again. Cook for another 5 minutes, so that both sides are rich, golden brown. Serve with sour cream or allow to cool to room temperature and then freeze.

Simon C. Garfield

Air Fried Cheese On Toast / Grilled Cheese

This is one of the classic comfort lunches, and it's super easy to make, even if you don't have many ingredients to hand. Forget boring cheese sandwiches; cheese on toast / grilled cheese is in a whole different league, and it's a fantastically simple thing to make in your air fryer. You can throw this together in less than 20 minutes, making it ideal for a quick lunch, and you can also add any variations you fancy. Love a bit of spice? Sprinkle some jalapeños in there. Fancy a salty kick? Try some slices of olive. In the mood for fish? A few tinned sardines make an excellent accompaniment. So, let's find out how to make grilled cheese!

SERVES: 1

You will need:

- 2 slices of cheddar cheese

- 2 teaspoons of butter

- 2 slices of bread

Nutritional info:

Calories: 341

Fat: 26.8 g

Cholesterol: 79 mg

Sodium: 525 mg

Carbohydrates: 9.5 g

Fibre: 0.4 g

Protein: 15.4 g

Simon C. Garfield

Method:

1. Preheat your air fryer to 175 degrees C / 350 degrees F.

2. Put your bread on a plate and butter one side of each slice. Make sure you get the butter right to the edges, because it provides the grease that will make the bread crispy and delicious.

3. Layer the cheese onto the bread, making sure that none sticks out of the edges. If you want other toppings, you can add them now. Mozzarella is a great way to make your sandwich stringy and melty.

4. Stick the two slices together. Place them in the air fryer and cook them for up to 8 minutes, until the cheese is gooey and completely melted.

5. Flip the sandwich over and cook it for another couple of minutes, and then take it out of the air fryer and serve hot. Allow to cool for a few minutes before eating as the cheese will be extremely hot.

Air Fried Mushrooms

If you've got some delicious portobello mushrooms ready to use, your air fryer can turn them from plain fungi into a succulent, rich meal. This recipe couldn't be simpler, and it's a great way to pack in some vegetables. You can eat these with any sauce or dip you enjoy, or load them up with a bit of sour cream or cream cheese. If you prefer spicy mushrooms, bump up the garlic and add a sprinkling of chilli powder across the tops.

SERVES: 2

You will need:

- 4 portobello mushrooms (or other large, flat mushrooms)
- 50 g / 1.7 oz butter
- 2 cloves of garlic
- 2 teaspoons of fresh tarragon

Nutritional info:

Calories: 205

Fat: 20.3 g

Cholesterol: 54 mg

Sodium: 145 mg

Carbohydrates: 3.3 g

Fibre: 0.1 g

Protein: 2.5 g

Method:

1. Preheat your air fryer to 180 degrees C / 350 degrees F.

2. Wash the mushrooms and set them aside to dry.

3. Mince your garlic and mix it into the butter.

4. Put the mushrooms with their gills facing up in the air fryer basket.

5. Mince the tarragon and sprinkle it across the gills, and then top it with garlic butter (this will melt in the air fryer, soaking into the mushrooms).

6. Cook for 5 minutes, checking halfway through. The mushrooms should turn golden and rich. Serve piping hot with a scoop of sour cream.

Vegetable Kebabs / Kebobs

Do you love grilled vegetables? If so, this is the perfect meal for you, and once more, it's totally adaptable to suit your favourite foods. You can make these with meat if you prefer, skewer a few prawns, or keep them vegetable-based. Serve them with any dipping sauce you like – but sweet chilli is a great option.

SERVES: 6

You will need:

- 3 red peppers

- 1 large onion

- 1 courgette / zucchini

- 1 teaspoon of garlic granules

- 2 tablespoons of vegetable oil

- 1 teaspoon of smoked paprika

- ½ teaspoon of red pepper flakes

- Salt

- Pepper

- 80 ml / 1/3 cup of your favourite dipping sauce

Nutritional info:

Calories: 77

Fat: 4.9 g

Cholesterol: 0 mg

Sodium: 33 mg

Carbohydrates: 8.4 g

Fibre: 1.9 g

Protein: 1.4 g

Method:

1. Wash your vegetables and cut them into large chunks so that they can be easily slotted onto the wooden skewers without a risk of them breaking.

2. Toss the vegetable pieces into a large mixing bowl, and add the chilli sauce (or other sauce), garlic granules, paprika, red pepper flakes, and vegetable oil. Mix well until all of the vegetables are thoroughly coated in oil.

3. Cover the bowl and allow the vegetables to marinate for around 30 minutes so that they soak in the flavours.

4. Preheat your air fryer to 200 degrees C / 400 degrees F and spray your air fryer basket lightly with cooking oil.

5. Slot your vegetable chunks onto wooden skewers, alternating to distribute the different flavours.

6. Space the skewers out in your air fryer basket so that the air can flow over them completely and then cook them for 5 minutes. Flip them carefully and cook for another 5 minutes so that the vegetables turn tender and crispy. If you have added meat, use a meat thermometer to check that it is cooked to the correct temperature.

7. Serve hot with extra sauce or some sour cream.

Conclusion

Hopefully, you now have a whole host of great recipes up your sleeve to make the most of your air fryer. This cooker is capable of doing so much more than chips / fries, so let its versatility shine and make use of it for any and every meal!

Whether you are making breakfast, lunch, or dinner, your air fryer can meet your needs, producing crispy, crunchy foods with a fraction of the oil in them every time. Air fryers are a great way to cut back on your intake of oil, and although you will still be using some fat for cooking, you can probably already see just what a difference this makes to your favourite recipes. This is both diet-friendly and wallet-friendly, because you won't be eating and wasting gallons of oil each year in order to enjoy your favourite foods.

Remember that your air fryer isn't just about making snacks; you can cook full meals in there, especially if you are prepared to do a bit of batch cooking. If you do need to cook in batches, use your oven on a low setting to keep the first few batches hot while you finish up the rest. This is a little frustrating sometimes, but it's the best way to make use of this gadget when you are cooking for a lot of people. Alternatively, use your air fryer for the sides and appetizers, and cook your main dishes in the oven.

Don't let your air fryer gather dust in the corner while you sit and wonder what to make. Whether you are preparing a great weekend breakfast for your kids or putting together a fancy meal for yourself and your partner, it is the perfect option. You can make vegetarian food, vegan food, meat-lover food – it's easy to create succulent dishes for any occasion.

Remember to clean your air fryer after each use, as soon as it has completely cooled down. This will ensure that it stays fresh and doesn't take on any odd smells. If you do notice that the basket or the pan have taken on an unpleasant aroma, soak them in lemon juice for a little while, and the fryer should be good to go again!

It's no wonder that air fryers have swept the nation in recent years; they offer financial savings, a reduction in waste, and a continuation of the delicious fried food that most of us have such a weakness for, without the associated health issues. What's not to love? Try out some of these recipes and make your air fryer your new best kitchen buddy.

EXCLUSIVE BONUS

40 Weight Loss Recipes

&

14 Days Meal Plan

Scan the QR-Code and receive
the FREE download:

Disclaimer

This book contains opinions and ideas of the author and is meant to teach the reader informative and helpful knowledge while due care should be taken by the user in the application of the information provided. The instructions and strategies are possibly not right for every reader and there is no guarantee that they work for everyone. Using this book and implementing the information/recipes therein contained is explicitly your own responsibility and risk. This work with all its contents, does not guarantee correctness, completion, quality or correctness of the provided information. Misinformation or misprints cannot be completely eliminated.

Simon C. Garfield

Printed in Great Britain
by Amazon

87483107R00064